RISE!

LEAN WITHIN YOUR INNER POWER & WISDOM™

Dear Ursula,
This book is written
by my friend
Uoselle who
accomplished his
amazing climb to
the peak!
    Love Brandl

RISE!

LEAN WITHIN YOUR INNER POWER & WISDOM™

MOZELLA PERRY ADEMILUYI

Rise! Lean Within Your Inner Power & Wisdom

For permissions contact:
info@mountainpeakstrategies.com

ISBN: 978-0-9819644-3-0

Cover Design:
Kerrianne Cartmer-Edwards,
Unforgettable Impact, Ltd.

ISBN: 978-0-9819644-3-0

DEDICATION

In gratitude to my parents,
Johnnie and Moses Perry -
my 'base camp'.

TABLE OF CONTENTS

Foreword by Cathy Hughes, Urban One, Inc.

FOREWORD

I give praise and thanks to God from Whom all blessings flow for my friend Mozella Perry Ademiluyi and her commitment to help everyone around her "Rise." Mozella is an author, international speaker and poet who continues to use her personal journey and life experiences to teach us how to live and become the best versions of ourselves. In the tradition of our motherland, Africa, where she spent a part of her formative years, she is a griot – one whose stories contain nuggets from which we can glean wisdom.

For many, mountain climbing is a metaphor that depicts the challenges of overcoming some of life's most insurmountable problems. For Mozella, however, her ascent to the top of Africa's highest peak, Mount Kilimanjaro, was much more. Not only was it a tribute to the parents who equipped her with the tenacity she needed to dare to do the impossible, but it also served as one of her greatest lessons as the mountain became her teacher.

On the pages of her latest book, "Rise," we become the students and recipients who benefit from all that great mountain had to teach her. "After walking up and down an endless number of hills on the first day, very quickly my master teacher reminded me of this: Each person's mountain has unexpected terrain that must be experienced as it is discovered and unfolds. Create the vision, set the goals, and then we each may have to adjust and redesign around what shows up in the middle of these plans." Mozella extracts practical applications like this from her climb atop the mountain's summit, at the youthful age of 60, and weaves them with anecdotes from her quest.

"Rise" will challenge you to look within and rediscover who you are. It will remind you not to "slow down when the going gets tough ... but to recognize the power in the pause – the ability to breathe, reboot, recharge and recommit." "Rise" will equip you with the useful skills necessary to set and accomplish your goals, overcome your failures and never be afraid to try again. And, most importantly, "Rise" will remind you that anything is possible and that you too can climb the Mount Kilimanjaros in your life.

Cathy Hughes
Founder & Chairperson
Urban One, Inc.

GRATITUDE FOR ...

It takes an amazing amount of support to write a book. I believe it could take pages if I were to move through the list of everyone who has impacted my life and ultimately contributed to *Rise!* You can well imagine.

Nevertheless, here is my attempt to do justice to the depth of gratitude I have for all of you.

I am grateful and blessed to have had a multitude of God given opportunities, beginning with my late parents, Johnnie and Moses Perry. I'd climb another mountain to honor you.

To my dearest family and friends who don't ever leave my side:

My best friend, Adegboyega A Ademiluyi, and your never-ending support; and, our sons, Yemi, Seyi, Toks, William and George, for being my constant cheerleaders. I don't know what I would do without my sisters Katherine Perry and Shirley Ford who walk all mountains with me; my brother Moses, Jr. who is my wise influencer; Gboyega Ademola (NY) for your defining role in helping me refine the title down to *Rise!*; Mandeep Chohan, my brave and adventurous childhood friend for saying 'yes' to our climb.

A very special thank you to Cathy Hughes. You've been an inspiration, friend, and mentor. I appreciate you.

Thank you, Carolyn Alexander, my high school friend for keeping me grounded with your clarity; and, my niece, Aisha Michael, for your creative touches.

Betsy McDowell for being an absolute God-send. Thanks for leading me through what it took to finish *Rise!* Without you... well, that's another story.

Katherine Perry and Zandra Faulks for your tireless questions, quest for clarity and edits and more edits.

Writing a book starts well before the first written words and moves beyond the finished product:

Jan Fox's pre-departure response to my journey "If you don't make it to the top, you don't have a story" went through my head more than once. My initial book coach, Ann Sheybani, who laid a tough, get it done foundation for how I approached what felt like a mountain of a task. It was. Thank you, Neil Gordon, for my homework assignments – they helped me crystalize the core message behind each and every step.

Kerrianne Cartmer-Edwards, your branding talents spilled over onto my book cover as well – you're a creative wiz.

Rekesha Pittman of Get Write Publishing - the famed Book Midwife for arriving just in time to guide the end process and assist in the delivery.

Thank you to our wonderful team who led us up Mt. Kilimanjaro - Summit Expedition & Nomadic Experiences. We believe you are the best on the mountain!

And last, but not least, the magnificent Mt. Kilimanjaro, a natural master teacher who patiently embraced my learning in ways only She could do.

INTRODUCTION

It's possible to reach your summit not when you accept what steps must be taken, but when you embrace them.

– Mozella Perry Ademiluyi

When I first decided to climb Mt. Kilimanjaro at the age of 50, my fears were greater than my dreams of achieving our goal. My sisters and I made it to just under 15,000 feet, exhausted and ready to head in the opposite direction of our ultimate goal. And yet, even as I turned back and did not reach the summit, I had experienced the groundwork for future success.

Mountains have been used as metaphors for eons. Whether you believe they represent difficulties or obstacles, opportunities or desires, the call to action is clear. To achieve the results you seek, you must *rise to the challenge*. Doing so will require ALL of yourself.

Rise! is an adventurous, empowering and systematic guide for the journeys that are before you. Whether in your personal or professional life, you will discover how to build and maintain the momentum to keep you moving from where you are, to the places you want to be.

We stand on the shoulders of those who believe in us. Like the African proverb, it takes a village to raise a child; we learn that no matter how good we are, or think we are, we live in an interdependent world. We need each other. It takes a team to climb a mountain™. Another popular African proverb says:

"If you want to go fast, go alone. If you want to go far, go together."

What follows are universal lessons I have experienced from the Nature Spirit of an influential master teacher, Mt. Kilimanjaro. She is the most beautiful nature sanctuary I have ever encountered. What was shared and synthesized, through my intimate relationship with this mountain, was meaningful, profound, and actually, beyond any adjectives I can use.

These lessons have coalesced into seven steps that call for us to *lean within* ourselves first because we are directly connected to an endless ocean of knowledge, creativity and wisdom. They are an invitation to renew our courage and beliefs. They are an invitation to fully embrace our paths by taking the required steps in whichever direction they may lead.

We walk through the experiences that help us achieve the extraordinary results we seek. Many of us have been told, and believe, that the answers to our questions are somewhere inside a vast space within, often called our Higher Self. We also know that our actions 'out there' impact our momentum. To reach our dreams and desires involves our hands and feet. It's a powerful system to absorb, integrate and activate.

For me, being inspired and challenged by nature's adventures is as intriguing as figuring out how to find the depths and heights within. Why? I get to explore who I am at my deepest levels by taking myself into an environment or space that requires more of me. These explorations include both intimate and expansive goals.

I can't get there without first imagining what I desire, making choices, connecting with empowering feelings, adjusting my beliefs and planning the steps I need to take. This is the inner game. This is what it means (and more), to *lean within*. Whether we are aware of it or not, our journey is lived from the inside out.

Mt. Kilimanjaro, in Tanzania, is one of the seven summits, the highest peak on the African continent, and the tallest freestanding mountain on earth. I had seen her as a child, and she first called me back 40 years later.

This natural master teacher offered me an experiential training grounded in ancient lessons. She demonstrated how our profoundly heartfelt thoughts create what we see in our physical realities; that the ultimate source of this powerful energy comes from somewhere beyond our understanding; and that the individual choices we make result in an infinite number of possibilities and outcomes.

In nature, all things have a purpose. The mountain symbolizes power, including the courage to stand alone. Metaphorically it is said that Mt. Kilimanjaro is the third planetary chakra. The third chakra represents the outflow that governs the power we have within and over our destinies.

This mountain experience emphasizes, for each of us, that without steady, progressive movements forward, results cannot be reached. Bold, consistent action is a critical part of the formula, but it is often the very part we fail to complete.

Mt. Kili provided challenging and rewarding lessons that synergistically pulled together so much of what I have learned and continue to learn. I share these lessons with you throughout this book.

BASE CAMP

**People do not decide
to become extraordinary.
They decide to accomplish
extraordinary things.**

– Sir Edmund Hillary

Our personal histories and stories help us understand our present. My late father's amazing story
is where my inspiration began:

He was born in Miami, Florida to parents of
moderate means. During his very early teenage
years in the 1940s, he had a fanciful idea to live
and work on the African continent.

For decades my father held onto what surely
felt like an impossible dream. He held on right
through the challenges of becoming a teenage
parent at the age of 17. He also held on right
through the rigors of university and through ten
years of his first major job as the Carver Branch
YMCA Executive Director in Miami, an assign-
ment he accepted after he finished his post
graduate work.

On October 9, 1962, my 33-year-old father left Miami to embark on the journey of a lifetime. With his wife and young family in tow, he set out for Jinja, Uganda, East Africa to live, work and fulfill his life's mission. What may have seemed to some a miraculous change in direction, was to my father a steady progression toward his dream. Our family would live between East and West Africa for the next 18 years.

People who mattered in his life were initially concerned about his outrageously bold and determined steps. Remember, this was the early 1960s. They questioned his judgment, or lack thereof. Well-meaning friends, family, and colleagues wondered how he could embark into the darkness of this unknown continent – with his young family! The Tarzan inspired images of Africa were prevalent at that time and fueled the naysayers' visions of man-eating lions and tribesmen.

If he had started by asking how his dreams were to unfold, or even what would happen as he set out on this new life path, he may have never left Florida.

He was a cutting-edge thinker and a pioneer. With a sense of awe, I finally understood this in later years. He opened the Jinja YMCA office with 'one table and a box to sit on.' I learned this detail thanks to the travel journal my mother kept.

Without his vision for a more dynamic future on a continent he had only read about, our lives would have gone in completely different directions and would not have been as enriched and full as they are. I know this to be true. Moving out of the United States literally opened us up to the entire world during our early, formative years. We became 'global citizens,' and this perspective has lasted throughout our lives.

My father left behind the momentous era of the civil rights movement in the United States to forge fully into the emerging, independent African countries. While masses of African Americans were migrating north, his hopes and dreams led him eastbound, across the expansive Atlantic Ocean. It was a huge leap of faith that took foresight and great courage. The results he sought were created by the persistent energy of his imagination, his actions, and the Universal Laws, which guide and support the threads that weave the tapestry of our lives.

My mother was 35 years old with three young girls ages six, eight, nine (that would be me), and a 16-year-old boy. Setting out, she was apprehensive, and yet had a sense of euphoria for the adventure that lay ahead. What a job to pack up an entire household and move so far away. I often wondered how she actually pulled it off.

Once there she adapted and entertained professionals from all over the world and managed to follow an intricate and completely foreign protocol. It had to have been a major learning curve because her world in East Africa had been nothing like her experience in the United States, where she was subject to a 'normal life' as defined by her social and church communities. Everything had indeed changed.

Again, thanks to my mother's travel journal and my father's 8mm movie camera, our family exodus was documented. She kept that journal from the moment we left Miami until she stopped (unfortunately) writing in it just two years later. She shared snippets of events I would have never recalled. For example, she documented the first time we saw and felt the African continent after touching down in Dakar, Senegal; the beautiful, exotic sights that greeted us; the rubber trees; the surprisingly modern buildings; and, of course, the heat.

After going to Monrovia, Liberia; Accra, Ghana; Addis Ababa, Ethiopia; and Nairobi, Kenya, we finally arrived in Entebbe, Uganda on October 29, 1962 – 20 life-changing days later. It had been an epic continental crossing.

The whole point of crossing the continent was to give my Dad insight into the cultures and YMCAs of other African countries. He was recruited to fulfill the pre-established purpose for the Jinja YMCA – youth development programs and vocational training.

I would never have been able to piece together these earlier, transformative years without the stories our parents shared with us, including mother's journal. This is the power of the written story. It holds history through the eyes of the storyteller for those who would either forget or who would never have known.

My memories of growing up in East Africa are a different set of stories for another time. However, when I was a child, we were always outside, climbing one thing or another. During high school in Kenya, hiking was a favorite weekend pastime. From our elevation overlooking the Great Rift Valley (our boarding school was called Rift Valley Academy) we could see Mt. Longonot and a most enchanting and calming landscape.

My love for the natural world developed early, and it continues to inform what unfolds in later chapters of my life.

This story and the many stories that I share here are part of the fabric of my life. It is when we tap into the strength of this web, that makes up the stories of our lives, that we have the capacity to not only change but transform what lies ahead.

Journaling your thoughts, direction, crossroads and decisions is a powerful tool: It is a reminder and a dependable guide when you've temporarily lost your way or don't know which way to turn. It tells you why you're there, where you've been, and will help you move forward too. It will inspire and reinspire you when you need it most. This book will highly encourage journaling, documenting your questions and answers.

The date of mother's very last entry formed the basis for our summit day, 50 years later. My sister and I chose the same day and month to mark and honor the anniversary of our parents' vision and courage. From the rooftop of Africa, on January 10, 2014, we held our handmade sign at 19,341 feet, and it simply read: Thank you Mother and Daddy Jan 10, 1964. My other sign, also made the night before our final ascent, proclaimed It's Possible. This sign was for us and it is for you too.

Martin Luther King, Jr. asked, "What is your life's blueprint?" and Abraham Lincoln said, "The best way to predict your future is to create it." Harry Belafonte challenged us to sing our songs.

The successes and lives of Cathy Hughes and Oprah Winfrey inspire us. They are examples of individuals whose inner power and determination fuel their deep desire to empower others.

My parents' influence, through quiet lives of service, continues to have a positive impact on the lives they touched. They followed a blueprint, created their future and most definitely they sang their song in the service of others. The life they created was the base camp from which my life experiences and life work evolved.

Becoming the person each of us is called to be, and most want to be, is about finding and moving toward and with our purpose. It calls upon us to hold our vision; find our team or our tribe; defy expectations; and, do those things that will move us to our goals and reasons for being here. It is up to us, even when we don't fully acknowledge it.

So, what makes this book different from the many personal and leadership development or transformational books you may have already read? Essentially, the answer lies in the chapters and nuances of my personal experiences with Mt. Kilimanjaro and how they apply to your experiences. Through what I share, my intent is that you will rediscover and recommit to the powers available within you. I trust it will encourage you to keep seeking and evolving in all the ways in which you can interact within this unfathomably abundant universe that is ours to explore.

Like me, you may have searched far and wide and ultimately learned that we must come back to ourselves first – who we are, what we are capable of achieving and how we get there. Sometimes in order to achieve one thing, we must go back and finish another. Sometimes, to prove to ourselves that we can, we must accomplish that which we fear.

My prayer is that you'll find *Rise!* to be a timely catalyst as you continue to find and navigate your course and achieve your goals and heart's desires. May it help to keep you, and/or your team, focused and aware. May it help you dive more deeply into an unfolding and molding of your own transformation.

Yes, the journey of a thousand miles does begin with the first step, so let's take it now and get started.

Step One

IMAGINE FIRST

We are most likely to achieve our goal when we focus not on our fear of failure but rather a vision of our success.

The poorest person in the world is not the one without money but the one without vision.

– Ghanaian Proverb

Mt. Kilimanjaro, "The Rooftop of Africa," towers above the Kilimanjaro National Park in Tanzania. Its base lies at about 2,600 feet of elevation and it soars to a height of 19,341 feet (3.5 miles). Of the three volcanic cones that comprise Kilimanjaro, Uhuru Peak is the highest summit on Kibo's crater rim.

I was 50 when I climbed Mt. Kilimanjaro for the first time. I set out, with my two sisters, Kat and Shirley, expecting that "we can do this." We made it a point to ensure that we had the right equipment, and we were decked out with most of the trappings of a successful expedition, or so we thought. Our preparation culminated in a huge send-off party with a cake in the shape of Mt. Kilimanjaro.

We set off on our adventure embracing that: "We were going to accomplish this feat – together."

After Day 1, my journal reflected a different tone:

"The terrain was more challenging than expected – figuring on not much incline in a rainforest. Didn't happen."

I consider myself a person with a fair amount of courage, however, on this journey, my can-do spirit seemed to whittle away rather rapidly. It started to dawn on me, that first day, that maybe we had taken on a challenge a wee bit bigger than we had foreseen. I had no way of knowing just how hard it would actually be, until we started out.

By the time Day 2 rolled around, the exquisite beauty of our surroundings were overshadowed by an increasing concern and fear that we were not going to make it.

On Day 3, of what was to be a five-day climb, we were doomed.

Kat had become ill from altitude sickness and we were tired and tense. We had hiked for over six hard hours barely placing one foot in front of the other. It was late in the day and we had at least two more hours to go in order to make it to our next campsite. Kat had "no power," to use her words.

We had long stopped looking at the mesmerizing beauty around us. This was getting serious and our hopes were now dashed against the large rocks ahead of us. Our guide requested an emergency crew via radio.

Although desperately hopeful, we were not absolutely certain when or if a stretcher was coming. It finally did – from up over the hill, six men ran down toward us. I almost cried with relief. We wanted it to be over.

Kat made the bumpy journey back, the way we had come, on the uncomfortable stretcher named "The Kilimanjaro Express." This left Shirley and me to walk back, with our guide, through hours of pitch-blackness with one flashlight between us. We retraced our steps back down to Horombo camp, deflated, despondent and exhausted.

We monitored Kat's fluids throughout an icy cold, shivery night. We were relieved to see the dawn arrive and she was again taken down for the final descent back to base camp. Shirley and I hiked another seven hours back down the mountain.

Although we hadn't made it to Uhuru Peak; we told ourselves that we had not failed. We had made it to just over the 14,500-foot mark, and more importantly we had learned some valuable lessons and enjoyed beautiful experiences during our mountain adventure.

Now, fast forward to January 2014. I'm 60 years old. My sister, Shirley, Mandeep, my childhood friend and I are about to attempt to climb

Mt. Kilimanjaro, (a second time for Shirley and me) after a 10-year hiatus.

One of the biggest differences between my first Kilimanjaro climb and my second was the change in how I approached the climb. The first time, I could not, did not see my sisters and myself making it to the top. Each day my primary focus and questions were fear-based concerns about whether I/we had what it took to reach our intended destination.

Fear-based images have tremendous influence over us. It's correct that we can't serve two masters at the same time. In this case it was fear or courage. At any given moment this choice shapes our lives. Choosing courage, when doom and gloom are all around, takes a very conscious decision to be and act differently.

In my poetry and prose book *Love Is A Mountain,* I shared:

> *During the moments after deciding to turn back,*
> *I felt strangely complete.*
> *After all, we had reached way up the mountain,*
> *though not to its highest peaks.*

Sometimes we are so busy trying to get to the top that we do not fully appreciate the altitudes and views that we do attain. Philosophically this is true, but we still hadn't made it, on that first ascent. We did not finish the way we had intended.

Something I discovered, from our first attempt, was that if we take time out to get over a failure or disappointment (coming back to where we believe we belong), trying again, or not trying again is a choice we make. Who among us hasn't hit a wall, missed our mark, or had to take the qualifying exam again? We seek the power within ourselves to BE more, to discover and uncover more of who we already are in the face of setbacks.

The goal is to be able to approach these setbacks in such a way that we are able to take the time to pick ourselves up, dust ourselves off, and try it again. We can ask ourselves what can we do differently to meet the challenges and opportunities before us?

The first step is to create a crystal-clear vision of our goal.

For many of us it's far too easy to try to "muscle" our way to an outcome. We think it's about resolve, force and willpower. The problem with how we typically achieve our goals is that we work hard and pound away, not truly knowing where we are going. Our journey is defined by obstacles. We are most likely to achieve our goal when we focus on our vision of success rather than on our fear of failure. A fearless imagination triggers success in whatever area of our lives we choose. For my Dad, it was exactly this level of vivid imagination, determination, and a deep self-belief that opened doors for him.

My dad knew he was Africa-bound. He just didn't know how or when he was going to get there. He did, however, keep putting one foot in front of the other until he made it to his goal – his peak.

During that first, aborted climb of Mt. Kili, I learned that without vision, without a clear picture of success, without moving past fear-based images, it is almost impossible to reach a goal.

In contrast to our first attempt, the story that led to our second attempt is much different. On December 4, 2013, one month before we started our second climb, I documented a reinvigorated belief system and determination in the journal I would take with me:

"Our sister Mt. Kilimanjaro is waiting for us – a vortex of energy we can learn and grow from. I ask that she impress her wisdom on our minds & hearts through the sights, sounds and experiences that wait for us. There is so much possibility in the vast realm of potentiality."

The poem I wrote further reflected my re-invigorated, lean within approach:

It's Possible!™
Open up your minds and attitudes
One day at a time,
One step at a time and
you will reach
where you're headed
A mountain, any mountain
a wonderful journey:
filled with gifts
and lessons
so analogous to life
preparation and planning
questioning yourself,
your intent and goals,
Setting out onto
the great unknown
path of discovery
If you weren't oh so afraid
that you might fail,
that you're too old
maybe too young
or seemingly-ill prepared,
The age-old question:
Do I really have
what it takes
Or …

Do I have what it
really takes?
It's Possible …
Four miles in the sky,
you say?

Yes,
It's possible!

We arrived at our base camp on January 2, 2014, and almost immediately this newfound resolve was put to the test. On Jan 3, 2014 at Mbaye Farm – a high-altitude coffee farm, I wrote:

> "We're as ready as we'll ever be. It's time now to work with whatever is before us – including the fact that Shirley's luggage won't arrive until tomorrow morning, the day our climb begins. This situation called on us to conjure up our best coping skills. It is amazing how quickly our enthusiasm is dampened at the slightest diversion – we are conditioned to believe that we need to have our way – that something is wrong when we don't."

Did I have to talk myself out of disappointment – even mild despair? Immediately! Although my sister's luggage delay caused us to start later than we had planned, I could see a clear view of Mt. Kili, and right from the start I pictured us at the top. I understood the importance of seeing this scenario over and over again.

When you're wondering and entertaining self-doubt, it's important to immediately call in the picture of what you desire. If you don't set an intention to stay focused and in the present moment, your mind could take you exactly where you don't want to go.

I also focused on the value of sharing my *rise to the challenge; lean within, and it's possible* messages with other women and how they could apply its inspiration in their own lives. I determined that each day I would continue to think about how I would share my experiences with those for whom mountains and other adventures could become their own metaphorical hero's journey.

Essentially, I added an altruistic element by imagining other women out there 'waiting for me to make it' so that they could benefit from my story too. So, I took them all with me. It became *our* climb and we all won, together. For me this was an empowering thought. It added even more fuel and kept me moving.

Admittedly, in spite of my brave front, I was nervous and full of excited anticipation. But, that's natural and a good thing – it got my blood flowing for what was to come. In this state of anticipation 'would we', and 'could we' were transformed into 'yes we can.'

Each one of us has experienced this level of focus and intent at some point in our lives. We want to know where we're going and why we're on the path. We want to believe. We want to know how to take decisive action. And, we want to have the resolve and courage to do so too. Even if we end up not being able to have it all, there's nothing wrong with wanting it all and going for whatever 'all' may mean to us.

After walking up and down an endless number of hills on the first day, very quickly my master teacher reminded me of this: Each person's mountain has unexpected terrain that must be experienced as it is discovered and unfolds. Create the vision, set the goals, and then we each may have to adjust and redesign around what shows up in the middle of these plans.

As I periodically looked back at the beautiful sights behind us and ahead at the exquisite landscape that was before us, we appeared to be in the middle of nowhere. Both perspectives reflected our progress.

RISE!

We stopped to appreciate the moments. "Wow, did we just do all that?" The key, though, was to stay present to the steps that were right in front of us. Yet, the expectation lay in keeping our inner eyes focused on where we were going. There would be some very long days ahead.

I kept in mind why I was there, while still enjoying the journey. There were times when I was surrounded by so much unusual foliage and natural beauty that it almost didn't matter why I was there. It was work and play all at the same time. The journey itself was filling me up, and, envisioning where I was going was part of that journey.

I know it may sound contradictory. However, it is a delicate balance between being present and yet keeping your eyes on the prize. The objective is not to dwell in the future, but to just make sure you visit it with the regularity required to keep you engaged with what you're doing and where you're going.

So, we moved beyond the rain forest, and then …

NOTES

_____

_____

_____

_____

_____

_____

_____

_____

Step Two

CHOOSE YOUR BOOTS

Your ability to take on monumental tasks is the result of having brought the proper tools to do so.

The journey of a thousand miles requires excellent boots.

– Mozella Perry Ademiluyi

Those who climb Mt. Kilimanjaro pass through five markedly distinct climate zones. These five zones are (from lowest to highest elevation): rain forest, heath, moorland, alpine desert, and the arctic zone. Each zone has its unique weather pattern. As climbers ascend the mountain, they move from the heat of the equator to an arctic freeze within a matter of days.

The second day of our ascent we forged ahead into the misty gusts of the heath zone. Here is where we first enjoyed the ethereal experience of walking through the moist clouds that floated around us.

This arid, rocky region was a stark contrast to the lush rainforests at the lower elevations. Here the sparse beauty of the landscape lies in the heather, exotic orchids, wildflowers and breathtaking blue skies.

Next, we entered the very enchanting moorland areas with its famous giant lobelias that look like giant cacti. The other-worldly moonscape of rock starkly contrasted with small bursts of floral color. Daytime mists are also common in the moorland, and nighttime temperatures are below freezing.

We eventually had to face the frigid alpine desert where not much can grow or survive. Here, the 40-degree fluctuation in temperature from day to night, lends itself to low growing ground cover, and scouring winds deter most plant and animal life.

Our journey ended in the arctic zone, which is graced by majestic, intimidating and massive glaciers.

Each of the fascinating zones presented us with the monumental task of moving with and through them. Each one was as unique as it was challenging.

On our second day on the mountain it became so much clearer that all our required equipment and proper clothes were not our most important tools. Our guides, John and Joel, porters, all 18 of them – the maps and our guidebooks, which told us where we were, where we were headed, and what to expect, made up the support that really mattered. This was the glue that kept everything together.

As I walked closely behind John, I synchronized my right and left footsteps with his. It just made sense. I found it simpler, and comforting, to follow and stay in step. The very intentional and slow rhythm, playing 'follow the leader,' kept my fatigue at bay as I knew what came after each step. It helped me stay on task and focused on what was directly before us.

We paused, periodically, to take in and renew our intentions with the 360° panoramic views. It was a stunning gift.

Sometimes I couldn't believe we were actually doing it – moving closer, and closer, and closer, and it was just our second day. I felt like we were explorers in the wild, wild, west because there was nothing out there but nature and us. The patterns of the landscape were etched in hills, valleys, more hills and more valleys and the singular lonely looking pathways that stretched as far as the eye could see. We were alone and it felt adventurous and intriguing.

It was a deeply satisfying feeling every time we turned to look back at how far we'd come in just a few concentrated and focused hours. We also paused because we were easily exhausted and needed a break from those arduous steps. Sometimes we wanted to stop but they gently pushed us a little farther before we could do so. It was a slow monotonous way of walking that everyone summed up in the words of advice "pole, pole" (pronounced polay, polay in Kiswahili) which means slowly, slowly.

When we did finally arrive at each campsite, the porters and cooks welcomed us with song, dance and celebration: "Jambo, Jambo Bwana, habari gani, mzuri sana ... hakuna matata." I will never forget the impact that their singing rituals had on us after each long, hard day of trekking. We would celebrate the day's achievements with laughter, and dance and let them take our backpacks as we began the process of releasing the discomforts and pain we had experienced during that day.

They all knew we needed to end each day with acknowledgement and gratitude for what had been accomplished. We celebrated with cups of hot chai, the real African chai, steaming with loads more milk than water, and a rich masala flavor, accompanied by a fluffy bowl of popcorn. What a deliciously odd combination it was that reminded me of our daily, childhood 'tea time' rituals.

Without the support of our team, we might as well have tried to climb without boots.

MY BOOTS

The ascent of Mt. Kili started well before we set foot on her. Those early challenges were just as crucial as the decisions that we were to make on the mountain.

I had gone in and out of sports equipment stores so often it was dizzying. All the details required attention. For example, the capacity of my backpack was an important detail. If it was too little, I would run out of space for daily necessities; if it was too big, I'd be more likely to stuff it with bits and pieces that didn't qualify as daily necessities and that would mean added weight I'd have to carry uphill. Not that our chief guide didn't have a say in what we packed before we even left for our base camp!

As I shopped for the required clothing, I was overwhelmed by a myriad of suggestions from sales people seeking to equip me with the very best.

Choosing my boots was the absolute hardest decision to make. "Are they really comfortable enough? Let me walk up and down the simulated path just one more time."

I knew this choice was critical. If blisters set in the consequences would be devastating. Sure, I could be proactive, by taping each and every toe and every hot spot I could identify. Which, of course, I did anyway. But, picking the right boots would spell the difference between feet that would make it vs. angry feet that would scream, "Stop!" at every challenging step. I had to get it right.

THE MAP

At Mbaye Farm, we poured over a map of our entire nine days during a pre-climb briefing with Wilson, a highly respected, retired guide. It was intimidating to absorb all that it would take; yet, we had to see the landscape in order to gain a sense of what our trek would entail. As Wilson explained, the route that we ultimately chose, the Lemosho route, was remote. We would be making an approach from the west; it had exquisite, scenic views; and, it was one of the more difficult, and less frequented of the seven available routes.

Choosing the Lemosho route meant we would face and climb the Great Barranco Wall.

Mt. Kilimanjaro has many breathtaking sights, and one of the most impressive is the Great Barranco Wall. With its steep cliffs, this imposing vertical rock face, rises 843 feet above the Barranco Valley, and has been framed in ominous terms by past trekkers.

Climbing the wall was slow going and arduous. You'll find out more about that in the steps to come.

It is here that we transitioned into the alpine desert zone.

NOTES

_____

_____

_____

_____

_____

_____

_____

Step Three

ATTITUDE
THEN ALTITUDE

It's not only our capacity but also our belief that defines our ability to move forward.

Your attitude is most empowered when you're determined to transcend, to climb beyond, whatever walls you perceive to be in your way.

– Mozella Perry Ademiluyi

Wilson, our second Mt. Kili pre-climb guide, required us to show him the contents of our backpacks for inspection. He knew what we carried in them would directly impact our ability to reach each day's goal. If it wasn't essential, or if it had the potential of weighing us down, we had to leave it behind.

In our briefing, Wilson told us that our mindset was a key success factor to achieving both a good trek and reaching the summit. I'll never forget how, after sharing stories about those who made it and those who didn't, Wilson simply asked: "Why shouldn't you be among those who make it?" He was right. He spoke of us reaching our goals, and he spoke of the act of actually getting there – the journey itself.

The first time we climbed, my journal was filled with worry about what the next day would hold. It was clear I wasn't sure we had what it would take to reach our goal:

I was "listening to the duality of dialogue going on in my head. There was fear, doubt and concern on the one hand – which was loud and clear ... as well as intention, determination and courage whose tone had a soft clarity to it. Positive & negative, cold & hot, fear & courage – these are the choices of internal dialogue ... particularly when there is a 'mountain' to face."

On September 23, 2003 at 12:35 a.m. I wrote: "It occurs to me – in a really practical sense – how much we'd prefer to 'pick and choose' our challenges if we could. We want it not too cold ... not too hot ... but just right!" From equatorial tropical to arctic wintry and back again ... in five days. The weather at Mt. Kili is said to be summer by day and winter by night."

During the first climb, my thoughts of doubt and fear ruled the wee hours of each night. I felt unprepared and inadequate simply because I had underestimated what it would take to accomplish our goal. I didn't know how to shift my thinking in the middle of it all.

My focus was on the fear of failure, not a vision of our success. I had missed the first and most important step – have a solid vision of success. There was even a tinge of relief when it became clear Kat could not safely continue the climb. I was exhausted and she became the 'out' that let me off the hook.

There was a kind of saved by the bell scenario for which I was unashamedly grateful. In a way our 'failure' was a blessing. In essence we hadn't even chosen our boots well. We didn't have the equipment we needed.

Imagine. We had arrived with no solid hiking poles thinking we could get them from the original company organizing our climb. Their paperwork had listed items that were available for our use. We should have known not to depend on them for such a critical item.

They loaned us one bamboo pole each. There was no way those would have been sufficient. They were not what we were expecting.

When it came to our clothing, we didn't have enough base layers, nor an adequate enough top layer for the glacier climate zone. We had not done enough homework. It was obvious, in hindsight, that we also hadn't equipped ourselves with the right mental attitudes and vision either.

Life can be a series of difficult climbs. On that first attempt, we were on one we were not ready for.

Contrast this earlier story to our second climb. The day before we began, I wrote: *"We can support each other's steps and thought patterns – we can remind ourselves that our open mindedness: our beliefs and attitudes will ensure we reach our intentions. It is possible and we will prove it to ourselves."*

By day 4, in spite of some sleepless nights, my mind was here: "It's very easy to go into fear mode because it can be so difficult, you don't feel all that well and you know there are harder challenges ahead. Having said that, I do believe that having made it through this day is a clear indication we are summit bound – successfully."

There's no question we had to push our way through. Each one of us had a fall; caught unaware by the slippery rocks below our feet. At one point, Shirley started to fight a cold and Mandeep teetered on complete exhaustion. I struggled too, yet we never considered turning back. I continued to focus on my breathing and my self-talk mantras. Each one of us was reciting whatever we had chosen to keep moving forward.

As individuals and as leaders we need to embrace both emotional and strategic agility. The demands of our lives can create physical burnout and make us feel increasingly isolated and impoverished.

Our life training rarely includes understanding the human needs that drive our behavior and determine our bottom line results. As individuals, we are more inclined toward exploring the zones of the heart as a significant player in our success.

In our professional lives, asking those deeper, emotional and psychological questions around what is driving our thoughts and behaviors has been an off-limits zone. Yet, companies and organizations wonder why efforts to increase employee productivity and engagement have failed. They fail to understand and implement this key principle of *Rise!:*

It's not only our capacity but also our belief that defines our ability to move forward.

My thoughts about what it took to get 'it' done were at their height on Kilimanjaro. She required more of us, and each of us, within the *substance* of our own mental chatter, had to have some positive repetitive thoughts that provided the fuel to do so.

The next step demonstrates how an empowered mindset can overcome limiting beliefs and help us move to where we want to be.

NOTES

_____

_____

_____

_____

_____

_____

_____

Step Four

CLIMB THE WALL

*We overcome the fears resulting from uncertainty
by celebrating incremental success.*

I learned that courage was not the absence of fear, but the triumph over it. The brave man is not he who does not feel afraid, but he who conquers that fear.

– Nelson Mandela

At this point in the ascent I came up against the dreaded Great Barranco Wall. The name itself made me shiver like the hyenas in The Lion King, who were terrified just calling the name, Mufasa.

Watching other people's experiences with this iconic obstacle, on YouTube videos, only reinforced my fears. It was one of the greatest question marks about our climb. Would we be successful getting up and over 'the wall?' Shudder.

I didn't need scary, powerful audio-visuals swirling around in my head, nor the messages: *'it's tough; you may not be able to make it over this hurdle. In fact, maybe you're really too old to be trying to climb Mt. Kilimanjaro again – what's wrong with you, wasn't 15,000 feet enough ten years ago?'*

This second attempt was costly: it could cost heartache and, yes, a little embarrassment too. Trying was a risk.

The spoken and unspoken thoughts of others can wreak havoc on your best efforts to stay the course. "What was she thinking of, why would she even bother again, what's she trying to prove?" All thought is powerful, for better or for worse.

Fear can cause a major collapse in confidence and make us question ourselves, again and again in corrosive and disempowering ways. When we need good positive news around us, why do we choose to focus on the negative? What makes bad news so attractive?

In hindsight, I often thought about the first trip and how that experience imploded on us in the end. The thoughts and feelings that I recorded in my journal during that failed attempt ranged from euphoria and confidence, to despair and fear and back to exuberance and awe again. I was unable to hold to my vision of success.

Theoretically, it's our fully committed, present thoughts that will impact tomorrow. Practically, when the present holds so much that is unknown, it takes an ongoing, day-to-day determination to hold to those yet to be realized goals and transform them into actionable steps.

I had written Tim Leinbach, the U.S. representative of SENE (the guide company we used) a million questions about "The Wall." I even considered changing our route in order to avoid the challenge "The Wall" represented in my mind.

Tim managed to get through to me, in one of his replies, with an assuredness that I could not fully grasp at the time. He wrote in large bold type "YOU WILL GET OVER THE WALL." He believed in my capacity to overcome this obstacle, and even though I didn't yet have that level of faith in myself, having his support and encouragement helped me move toward what I wanted to accomplish.

The wall was never far from my thoughts. Once the actual trek had started, doubt started to creep in again and find voice in my fear. John, our chief guide, said very kindly, "Mozella, the wall is four days away, we'll deal with the wall when we get there." I had been poised to spend three days creating stories and anticipating an outcome for an event that hadn't even begun. As a result of that advice I didn't take it off the stove, but I did place it on a back burner.

Finally, on day four, January 7th, we were facing what the famous, no nonsense trek author, Henry Stedman, called 'the breakfast wall.' Why? Because you climb it right after an early morning breakfast and the sheer effort and fear of it often has climbers spewing their breakfast all over it. Ugh! That information alone was one more non-supportive 'thing' that swirled around in my head. But it was too late, like negative news just before bedtime, it was out, and now I had to think about that too.

I couldn't believe how hard it was. It was the first place on our journey that we had to crawl on all fours. Given the entire ascent, it was the only place someone had to help us, physically help us land as we leapt from one rocky ledge to the 'safety' of another. I found myself thinking that I must have lost my mind – what was I doing up there – looking up was terrifying – looking down wasn't even a consideration. I'm cautious around heights and couldn't face seeing how far we were climbing up this 800 plus foot rocky wall that I now felt, for sure, wasn't intended for me. Falling was possible and of course others have been injured on that very wall. I didn't dare over think it. I had to make it; entertaining any other thought was too terrifying.

It took a massive effort to keep going. *As if I really had a choice.* My thoughts bounced back and forth between the consequences of failure and a "please help me God" kind of prayer. *If I make it up this wall,* and yes, in spite of it all I knew I would, *I promised never to be afraid of anything again.*

47

I just knew that this had to be the most challenging moment of my life – what could be worse? And, if I could accomplish this feat, I could accomplish anything.

It took longer than they said it would; however, we made it. I felt relieved and grateful for being able to finish something that hard. I used every bit of strength I had to pull this one off. Surely nothing could be harder – at least so I thought, until the final ascent day, but more on that later.

This challenge underlined the lesson that things change, and we have to adjust accordingly. On the way up The Great Barranco Wall, I did not have the time to think about anything apart from the one place I needed to put each hand and foot. The imperative was such that nothing else entered my mind. I had to focus on each step before I was in a position to take the next, and the next.

Did we need to take frequent rests and breaks between the steps? Absolutely.

Most of us need breaks when faced with particularly challenging tasks. Other hikers may have been able to climb faster. Our porters were certainly adept at coordinating their hands and feet and moved at what appeared to be an effortless pace.

Even though an entire journey still stretched out before us, the moment we actually faced that wall was the only moment that mattered. The commitment and effort we needed called for total focus and concentration. We believed in our capacity to take the next step, and then the next step. We trusted our guides, our preparation and, ultimately, ourselves. This fueled our forward momentum and, our ultimate success.

CONFIDENCE

We want to know what is behind our fears and our walls. Most often it is the lack of confidence. Confidence is the antithesis of fear. When we develop confidence, we minimize fear. Being sure of me, feeling confident in who I am, where I've been and what I have to share has been a long uphill battle.

I remember the feeling of not having any confidence from a young age, more specifically, from the moment I stepped into Victoria Nile School in Jinja, Uganda. I was 9 years old and lost in an academic world that was largely beyond my comfort zone and experience. Well, except for English and Literature, which I devoured like candy. I loved to read all kinds of books and poetry.

On the other hand, I shunned anything mathematical. I felt like the class dunce. I felt exposed during exam times when my lack of math skills would be open for all to see. Exam results were displayed publicly on bulletin boards.

I learned to become insular in the classroom and avoided speaking out unless I absolutely had to. Our fears and insecurities often have deeper roots than we are aware. A little sleuthing and we can generally figure out where 'that' came from.

In spite of being in an African country, being black was ironically reason enough to standout in a sea of white faces at our schools. Being American sometimes added insult to injury. It was often hard, and the sinkhole created by my lack of confidence was becoming deeper and would prove to be a difficult one to climb out of.

Standing out took an emotional toll that stayed with me throughout much of my education abroad.

It became particularly challenging when I left middle school at Loreto Convent in Eldoret, Kenya and transferred to an American based education, just outside Nairobi, Kenya. The white American missionaries were a massive wake up call. The hypocrisies, and racial and religious discriminations I witnessed built up a resentment that took years to overcome.

I faced many challenges in adapting to different cultures, schools and lifestyles. These represented walls that I would eventually have to scale. Change can be scary.

Our childhood and young adult stories form an undeniable foundation for who we think we are in the years that follow. These stories can silence our growth or greatly expand our reach depending on where we were, what experiences were before us and how we interpreted them.

What helped me turn the corner was the choice I made in attending Howard University; although, I became aware of a degree of separation there as well. Most students were empowered by the black power era, yet many others wanted very little interaction with the 'over-enthusiastic students from Africa.' Ultimately, Howard balanced my experiences of racism by adding a layer of prejudice that existed among African Americans and students from the African continent.

Climb the Wall is a symbolic example of how our inner fears, misunderstandings and doubts can distort our experiences.

NOTES

_____

_____

_____

_____

_____

_____

_____

Step Five

REALIGN WITH THE STEPS

The more daunting a task, the more we benefit from realigning ourselves to it.

Focusing on each and every step you take on any of life's treks reveals the essence of the work that is yours to do.

– Mozella Perry Ademiluyi

Navigating each step on your path helps you meet the next one and the next one with a great deal more confidence. Sometimes we do fall.

I have fallen many times, in many ways. When I fell on Kili, I was surprised because I thought I was being so careful. The area we were in had a considerable amount of scree, the small loose stones found on the slopes of mountains. When you are aware of potential hazards, like frozen black ice, your warning antennas go up.

Shirley and Mandeep had both fallen earlier, and that should have been my warning to pay attention, but I fell anyway. I picked myself up and brushed myself off, tended to my *slightly bruised feelings and minor discomforts,* took a break and then we kept moving. You can count on falling. So, it's best to develop the capacity to recover from a fall so that you can count on this ability to get back up, as well.

I had spent far more time *worrying* about missteps than actually having them. Worry is counterproductive. It makes us too cautious and actually slows us down.

The terrain kept me on my toes. I understood. My doubt didn't disappear, but on the second attempt I had better tools to overcome them. Yes, it took a different effort, not more effort, and it was all systems go, The Great Barranco Wall and all.

Remember, everything counts, and we always learn *something*. It's this 'learning something' that helped me become even more keenly aware of all that my mountain was sharing. Each area had its own stunning beauty that spoke and whispered volumes. Walking in alignment with what was in my immediate circle of experience kept me connected to what movement was required and what thoughts I needed to focus on to get there.

STEPS TO HELP YOU EMBRACE TAKING ACTION

Many people give up on their goals because it is simply too 'hard' or demanding to achieve them. They don't have a team of cheerleaders. Their belief systems don't sufficiently support them either. This is why sticking to new habits is such a challenge. People on diets and fitness programs stop doing the work.

Taking repetitive steps toward a goal is tedious work, and, we fall more often than we would like to admit. This is why the emphasis on daily steps is so critical. No matter how boring or endless they may be; the way to align and realign with them is to pause, look around at how far you've come, celebrate, and then keep moving forward.

Being sure-footed is also about paying attention and maintaining the right vision, intention and attitude. You will always benefit from spending time in thought and prayer about where you're headed and why it matters that you get there.

In walking meditative mode, I was able to prayerfully repeat messages that affirmed a "can do" spirit. It was freeing in many ways. It was like a walking pilgrimage.

My thoughts weren't about what was down the road, they were about the steps that made up my present moment – I can't repeat this point enough. Without this philosophy, it's so much easier to stumble and fall. It's about taking the process and breaking it down; taking this journey and this path and breaking it down to this step and then this step, while monitoring this thought and then this thought.

It's like Ann Sheybani, my "first phase, no-nonsense, get it done now book coach" advises in her book *How to Eat the Elephant: Build Your Book in Bite-Sized Steps* – "You know better than to contemplate massive goals in their entirety." My contemplation was centered only around the parts of that journey that were before me. I didn't dare think or look too far ahead at the massive goal before us. Lean Within!

STARTING

Juxtaposing my desire to move enthusiastically into an adventure with the cloud of fear that filled my thoughts, and that sometimes over-shadowed it, was not new to me. At 56, I was in Peru on vacation. My experience with the famed Machu Picchu mountain proved to lay the groundwork for what was to transpire on Kili-manjaro.

I remember the moment I decided to climb Machu Picchu. It was in September 2009 and my husband, Gboyega and I were touring that iconic area that most people recognize as Machu Picchu. You know the picture I mean, the mountain and the beautiful ruins around it. Our guide pointed to the mountain and said, "Everyone thinks this is Machu Picchu." Then he turned around (which we all did), and pointed, "*that* is Machu Picchu!" I gasped as I gazed upward, much higher than where we stood. Soaring above us was the famous mountain. I could see the flag, at its top, flying from a distance.

On that excursion I did not bring proper hiking boots as I originally had no intention of doing any serious climbing. What our guide did share was that it was challenging, and few people chose to take it on. The "mistaken identity mountain" was actually called Huayna Picchu, and it had several hundred people lining up to climb it every day. The real Machu Picchu received fewer than a dozen climbers a day.

At that very moment I knew I had to go. I went back to our hotel and called the front desk, organized a last-minute guide, and left the next morning. I had barely stepped onto the rugged trail before I started to panic. My breathing was labored, and my chest was tight. My heart and mind were racing, and I was panting just getting to the actual starting point. What did this mean for the success of what was before me?

I certainly wasn't embracing the steps before me. Rather, I was wondering if I had lost my mind.

In an odd way I felt silly. What made me think that I could tackle this challenge with no practice or preparation? Doubt set in, as doubt does when you don't have all your ducks in a row.

Starting can be the most difficult part of any journey. You know where you intend to go, you're just not sure if you can get there. I knew where I wanted to go, I wasn't sure I had what it took to get there. Does that sound familiar? That sense of not being enough because you're not ready? I know it well.

First thing I had to do was to calm my nerves, I did. I talked to myself for the next 20 minutes or so because I had to change my expectations if I was going to get anywhere.

I felt like I was in an exam and I had just over four hours to pass it. As I've shared, and again can't say enough, starting can simply mean putting one foot in front of the other until you know you're doing 'the thing' and then realize that every action is in fact taking you closer. This drives home the point that developing the habit of starting out on your mountain, each and every day, is imperative to your success.

An endless set of steps, built by the Incas of long ago, became a focal point as each one reminded me of the sage advice that a journey of a thousand miles begins with the first step. What I realized was that I had been taking this same course with the same lessons, over and over again, for some time.

Staying close to a wall on Machu Picchu, as I worked my way around the most dangerous part of the climb, became practice for handling my fears. You may have to slow down when the going gets tough, however, you must keep moving. Small trees became 'my friends' as I used them to pull me up. My guide became my coach as he reminded me that I was capable, and I'm delighted to share that I made it to the top of Machu Picchu's stunning peak.

You're rarely alone on your mountain. You'll find the help you need when you ask for it. It usually appears when you require it the most.

ENDLESS JOURNEY

Each day on Mt. Kilimanjaro felt epic. If we stared long and hard enough, we could sometimes see the tiny outline of a trail of ants, fellow trekkers that were making their way through the endless landscape. It would take continuous heroic output to get to where we were going. The distances we saw on the horizon looked insurmountable and yet we knew, that somehow, we must get there. One of the most amazing aspects of being on something as huge as a mountain is the awareness of how small we are in comparison to this vortex that seems to swallow us up from all sides.

The pathway ahead can appear so far away; so impossible without the aid of a vehicle or something that transports you to your destination much faster. You may feel it is pointless to be out there attempting the impossible. Then, you place your feet on the day's path and begin to move forward, yet again. Pole, pole (remember, in Kiswahili means slowly, slowly).

Everything matters when you are aligned with your steps.

As we traversed the arid landscape, at the higher elevations, I noticed occasional spots where springs came up from the ground offering a water source for the few plants and animals that survived there. I asked John, our guide, about these oases. He confirmed that the porters, who were far ahead of us, would fill their buckets at these spots, load them onto their heads, and carry them to the next campsite. This was water that would be treated, and made safe for drinking. This was water that would be warmed and provided in the small bowls that were offered us to wash off the day's dust and dirt.

The beauty of the panorama that unfolded around us took our breath away; that and the diminished supply of oxygen at the higher altitudes saw us walking in silence, and it was that struggle to breathe that often took precedence. The struggle to maintain forward momentum often held our focus.

'Endless' may sound tiring. It is and it isn't. On the one hand, you feel like you'll never get there. On the other hand, despite the exhaustion, it is doable because others have gotten 'there' and you can too. Metaphorically, our campsites, and home base nourish and hold us safely through challenging times.

The Imperative of Pause

Know when and where to pause each day and you will have the much-needed break just when you think you can't possibly take another step.

Stopping as often as our guides would allow, which was more often than they would have liked, gave us a chance to distract ourselves. We would devour the little sweet treats we had brought along. Mandeep had a stash of toffees that made all the difference to the quality of our breaks.

More often than not, our stops provided the temporary relief from the ongoing, nagging bouts of exhaustion we felt. John was particularly concerned about Mandeep as, unlike Shirley and I, she had not taken the anti-altitude sickness medication. Eventually, she had to do so and it made all the difference from then on. In spite of whatever stops were needed, at least there was the support of meds that put her out of the danger zone.

Pausing also allowed us to drink in the unique beauty that we would not see again. Although the end of the breaks that we took meant getting right back into the demanding requirements of making progress, we always managed to set out again with just enough renewal to make it to the next break.

Our campsite was as important as the details of our day's trek. Without it, our capacity to renew our energy, required to get us through the subsequent days, would have been hindered.

LOST IN SPACE

When we climbed Mt. Kilimanjaro, there was no getting lost. Instead, there was a clearly defined daily plan of action. We *were* going to meet our goals unless we chose to abandon (or couldn't continue) the entire expedition itself.

Not so when I hiked the 192-mile Wainwright Coast to Coast walk across England in 2015. I had two other wonderful companions, my adopted son, William, and a dear friend, Jodi. We had a junk compass we couldn't read, maps that confused us, and no guide. Yes, we got lost multiple times.

Actually, we were following Henry Stedman's guidebook, (yes, Henry, again) on how to navigate the vast terrain we were crossing. His book had been written years before our trek. Paths change slightly. A highway is built. Markers get destroyed. Yes, this is a caveat to exclusively following someone else's plan, without any other backup or ideas about what *you're* doing out there.

I particularly remember one time when we huddled over the guidebook and decided to take a course of action that we believed was the right way. It entailed crossing over a narrow rapidly flowing river – each one of us had to find the spot that we felt was doable for us.

It took me a while. I couldn't find the rocky supports that I felt would keep me from landing in the water. Once on the other side, we resumed our trek. Ten minutes into it, coming down a hill, we saw two hikers headed toward us. Horrified, we discover that we weren't on the Coast-to-Coast route. We had to retrace our steps, which included going back over the river that had caused me so much anxiety. That entire initial effort had been in vain.

Much more apprehensively, I made my way back. And, just before I was about to step up onto the river bank, I took a panicked misstep and my foot slipped into the water.

With one very soaked shoe, we now had to face where we should have been; an incredibly scary, steep hill of stairs they called "the stairway to heaven."

Clearly the above story demonstrates how you don't want to be on your journey. Being clear about where you are going is critical to your ability to face the fear and do it anyway. Doubt, brought on by not having sufficient understanding of what is needed and how to navigate the path ahead, can cause us to second guess ourselves. Doubt can become like a giant fog bank that we can get lost in, wandering aimlessly. Doubt is the precursor to panic, and panic opens the door to fear.

There are several possible reasons for being lost. You don't have a map, and then, to add insult to injury, you find yourself swept way off course by the first strong wind, and no way to get back. You need to take a breather, and, yes, actually breathe. Or, you're stuck. And, if you're stuck, really stuck, you might need to assess exactly what this means and where you are.

NOTES

_____

_____

_____

_____

_____

_____

_____

_____

Step Six

ASSESS YOUR PLATEAU

Plateaus are an opportunity for determining why we are where we are.

When the music changes so does the dance.

– African Proverb

After two full days of hiking, we reached the Shira Plateau, an 8 mile stretch that is one of the highest pieces of flat land on earth. Who would have thought that after all that climbing, we would have an opportunity to spend a little downtime on a plateau? It felt like a very special gift, giving our legs a much-needed change and breather. The beautiful flora went on for what felt like days.

We were walking on the remains of a collapsed volcanic crater. It was meditative for what lay ahead. It was also a yipeeee! moment, we looked all around, – *now*, where are we? And, how long will *this* last? We enjoyed the time, and got to walk faster, which was a welcomed pace.

To understand the impact the Shira Plateau had on us is to understand the feelings we had prior to arriving there. I'm sure Wilson must have told us about the plateau. However, I believe that the tough day-to-day physical challenge and the impact of the Great Barranco Wall had blotted out any thoughts of the gift that lay just beyond. The plateau made me feel like I needed to linger far longer than it took us to walk through this area. It made facing the remaining challenges that much harder.

We had made our way through as many emotional zones as we had climate zones. The transitions weren't always easy.

At base camp and in the rainforest, we were excited and full of anticipation. As we slowly ascended, the increase in altitude, exertion, and ongoing challenges took their toll on us. We welcomed what we saw and experienced, yet there was the continuous emotional pull between the two poles of conflicting belief systems.

I sometimes felt that the more the landscape and air thinned out, the more threatened my open mindedness was in response to the changes that were before me. It's a balancing act to believe one thing and experience another.

You often hear that the closer you get to the finish line, the harder the task becomes. So, reaching the plateau was both a blessing and a curse. The latter because we knew it couldn't last; it somewhat dampened our willingness to move along to the harder parts that lay ahead.

Sometimes loosening your drive to move forward gives you a break, sometimes it makes you wonder the extent to which you actually have the capacity to push ahead to the next big hurdle.

When we think "plateau" we most often think *stuck, fixed* even *failing to grow* or *not getting anywhere*. Yes, it can mean that; however, it can also mean the very opposite. Working day in, and day out toward your goal is demanding and takes a tremendous number of hard-earned hours.

Ultimately, I walked through the Shira Plateau with an immense sense of appreciation for what it did for me and for all of us. Of all the experiences that the vastly different environments had provided, this one allowed us to stop our racing minds and pounding hearts and temporarily relax our stressed bodies. It gave us time for laughter and gratitude. It was a time for me to further store up the mental, emotional and physical fuel that it would take to complete what we had all come to accomplish.

The plateau was an opportunity to turn my attention to my mind and it allowed me to be introspective about the encouragement I required. The break was also a welcomed invitation to rest.

It made me realize that we all need a Shira Plateau in our lives. I certainly needed that one. It came sandwiched between two opposite poles. It made me realize the true value of breaking momentum. Although on the one hand I wondered how I would react to the need to shift back into a more demanding gear; on the other hand, I recognized the power in the pause.

The ability to breathe, reboot, recharge and recommit was worth the momentary disruption in our previous work flow and demands. It allowed us to both fully lean within and tap into our internal resources, and, it empowered us to rise to the challenge and face the ongoing agenda that moved us closer to where we deserved to be.

I felt free.

NOTES

Step Seven

LOOK BEYOND
THE SUMMIT

*By committing to continuous growth,
you will achieve not just a good result
but also an extraordinary one.*

**Don't ever forget why you're doing what
you're doing. It provides the fuel
that keeps you moving forward.**

– Mozella Perry Ademiluyi

On January 10, 2014, we began our summit day at 4:00 a.m. It was dark, very cold and I was cautious and really apprehensive due to the clusters of rock walls and steep terrain we encountered right after leaving camp. I like to see where I'm going, especially if there is a possibility of falling. I like to know what's around and below me. This morning was not like that. It was a tedious, demanding and frightening start. And I was so grateful for the light that the sunrise eventually brought to us after our first two hours.

After days of trekking through the beautiful and stunning terrain that seemed to go on into eternity, we spent our last hours in a barren looking land. The arctic desert was guarded and intimidating. There were rocks and more rocks.

It was becoming colder and our brief, and now more frequent stops, were no longer refreshing. John and Joel did, however, give us short, coveted moments to regroup and attempt to inhale whatever oxygen was available in the thinning air. It was here that we were most challenged.

Our guides were keenly aware of how we were feeling and responded to every pronounced step we would make. Inside, I held my repeated belief that we would make it to the top, yet I wasn't sure *how* we would accomplish this task, as every step had become an even more immense effort with very little reprieve in between. It was incredibly hard. What was typically described as a six-hour final ascent, actually took us nine long hours.

When we were closer to the Stella Point Summit, John reminded us that we could stop there, take a few pictures and turn back down the mountain. He said most people do just that and that there was no need to push for Uhuru Peak. He clearly believed we had reached our limits.

My exhausted, yet determined response was: we had come that far and reaching Mt. Kilimanjaro's peak remained our goal. I didn't want to stop short of our goal because *he* was willing to let us off the hook.

Sometimes others see you struggle, and, because of their compassion, they tell you it's okay to be satisfied with where you are, that you don't need to work so hard to achieve more. They encourage you to stop right where you are, be satisfied or even turn back.

We chose to move forward. We intentionally passed up the photo op. No picture taking at Stella Point – it would have taken far too much of the energy that was required to keep us moving toward the peak. Every labored step was a phenomenal effort. I couldn't have foreseen what our climb would require of us. I'd never put out so much energy.

In those last moments, gasping for limited oxygen was our predominant focus. With each step, the effort was to take in whatever was there. All doubts were overcome by our labored but determined effort, because, in spite of how we felt, we just kept moving.

And finally, I looked up and I could see the end. The flags, the sign and the celebration of a massive accomplishment were all waiting. The feeling was great.

I knew we had arrived, even as we kept moving until we actually got there. As we inched closer, my frozen tears of sheer joy and relief had nowhere to go. An immense pride was rising up within me. I was so grateful that we had done what we said we could and would do. I will never forget how I felt as I made those last few steps before standing on top of Uhuru Peak.

By committing to continuous growth, you will achieve not just a good result but an extraordinary one.

Summiting Uhuru Peak unleashed an amazing amount of strength within us. We were striking energetic poses as if the whole thing had been a breeze. We high-fived each other. We had done it!

We sat for a few minutes to take it all in. In spite of some doubts and concerns along the way, the vision I had seen so clearly had come true. We were on the rooftop of the African continent, astride its highest peak.

Shirley and I took a picture with a sign that read "Thank you Mother & Daddy Jan 10 1964." Our planned arrival date at the peak was a tribute to our parents and coincided with the date in Mother's travel journal that documented the first time we had ever set eyes on Mt. Kilimanjaro. The significance, pride and joy of revisiting her, in this way, 50 years later was humbling.

In one picture, I held a sign that simply read, "It's Possible." This was a pivotal moment in my life where I also celebrated being enough.

We were not able to stay much longer at that altitude and had to prepare for the journey back to our campsite. In stark contrast to the climb, our demanding descent was like a nauseating, fast-paced roller coaster ride that was aimed to get us back down to a safer altitude as quickly as possible.

Many hours later, our porters danced and welcomed us home one more time as if we had won Olympic Gold medals.

We had!

NOTES

_____

_____

_____

_____

_____

_____

_____

EPILOGUE

People often share that they could never face the mountains that I have climbed. And I think to myself, "you're facing them all the time." It's no wonder that mountains are an old and immensely popular metaphor for life. They represent opportunities, challenges, and everything in between.

When you've moved past an obstacle and achieved the exceptional results you are seeking – or when you may have missed the mark entirely, there is always more. It's the nature of life that we keep desiring more. It's the nature of life that we are constantly creating, whether we do so consciously or not.

As we become more aware of what it takes to move through the journey from where we are to where we are destined to be, the teaching stories that are within my story, our story, is a reminder to use your conscious and creative powers of imagination to choose which road(s) you will take.

To help you further integrate what we have covered here; I invite you to take yet another step that will encourage you to lean within and connect more deeply. Access the *Rise! Guidebook* at:

www.MountainPeakStrategies.com/Rise

When you take those bite-sized pieces, and embrace the steps we spoke of, you will make the changes and create the transformation that you, and your team, desire. These goals can be actualized through the vision, thoughts, mindset and actions that we have discussed throughout this book. Synergistic alignment of these key pieces is critical. It is doable.

Remember, what applies personally can have a domino effect on the outcomes experienced within a team of people. When empowered leaders and teams are created, then the heights to which they and their organization or corporation can soar are limited only by their definition of success.

It has been my honor to walk this walk with you. For more information on It Takes A Team to Climb A Mountain workshops, please contact us at **info@mountainpeakstrategies.com**.

Play with the pieces, place your goals on the mountaintop of your dreams. Take one step forward at a time, and you will reach your destination.

As Nelson Mandela shared:

**"After climbing a great hill,
one only finds that there are many
more hills to climb."**

CLIMB ONWARD!

LEAN WITHIN!

RISE!

BOOKS AND RESOURCES THAT HAVE ENRICHED MY LIFE

These are a Few of My Favorite Things:

The Power of Imagination, The Neville Goddard Treasury

Choosing Happiness, Stephanie Dowrick

Goddesses Never Age, Christiane Northrup, MD

Long Walk to Freedom, Nelson Mandela

Working with the Law, Raymond Holliwell

The Science of Mind, Ernest Holmes

I Know Why the Caged Bird Sings, Maya Angelou

Abundance Now, Lisa Nichols

Soulcraft, Bill Plotkin

Power Thinking,
http://www.Paraliminal.com/MPS

The Way of Mastery, Shanti Christo Foundation

Breaking the Habit of Being Yourself, Dr. Joe
Dispenza

Things Fall Apart, Chinua Achebe

The Golden Book of Fairy Tales

Longing for Darkness, Kamante's Tales

Crossing the Unknown Sea, David Whyte

Power vs. Force, Dr. David R. Hawkins

The Answer to How Is Yes: Acting on What Matters,
Peter Block

Global Mind Change, Willis Harman

Sing Your Song, Harry Belafonte

Love Is A Mountain, Mozella Perry Ademiluyi

ABOUT MOZELLA

Mozella's gift for helping others navigate creative new paths originated in her childhood. When she was nine, she and her family moved from Miami, Florida, to the African continent to fulfill her father's lifelong dream. A passionate world traveler to this day, she brings her deeply-wired global perspective and cultural appreciation everywhere she goes and to everyone she meets.

An international speaker, author and poet, Mozella earned her undergraduate and law degrees from Howard University. She is a member of the Bars of the District of Columbia Court of Appeals, the Federal Republic of Nigeria, and is admitted to practice before the

United States Court of International Trade. She is also Founder of Rising Sun Programs, a non-profit organization that teaches young people and their families how to achieve personal and financial well-being through wealth literacy[SM].

Mozella is married with three grown sons and lives in Potomac, Maryland.

WORK WITH MOZELLA

Mozella leads women through transformative and executive leadership retreats. To find out more about these immersion adventures, go to:

https://www.loveisamountain.com/seasonal -retreats/

Mozella facilitates innovative workshops that guide individuals, leaders and their teams toward a better understanding of how attaining important goals, like climbing mountains, is best achieved when each person is fully prepared, engaged and responsible. When a critical mass of empowered individuals has been reached, and when the team believes and can articulate the concepts that fuel their aspirations, then the heights to which they and their company soar are limited only by their definition of success.

http://www.mountainpeakstrategies.com/work-with-mozella-workshops

Mozella created **Global Women Story Circle** (GWSC) as a singular online community that encourages women around the world to express their voices and discover the power of their own stories.

https://www.loveisamountain.com/global-women-story-circle/

Now Is the Time – 52 Weeks on Your Mountain is an interactive journal that you begin at any time. Over a period of 52 weeks, you are invited to move through a fun, and rewarding journey. Like mountain hiking, you need to take one step at a time. It will help you focus on your desires and longings. This journey will help you get closer to where you are headed and is designed to encourage you to lead yourself on a daily, weekly, moment by moment adventure touching just about every aspect of your life.

https://www.journal.loveisamountain.com

PHOTOS

Our Mountain dining room

Cooks in the 'kitchen'

The kitchen tent

Porters celebrating

The final approach

With our guides

A Tribute to Our Parents

Mission Accomplished

Inca Trail on Machu Picchu

Machu Picchu summit

Reflections on Machu Picchu summit

Made in the USA
Middletown, DE
05 November 2019